When Life Gives You Lemons...

and other recipes for living and loving life

HAZELDEN®
Keep Coming Back™

Created by Meiji Stewart

Illustrated by David Blaisdell

When Life Gives You Lemons...
© 1996 by Meiji Stewart

ISBN# 1-56838-381-9

Hazelden
P.O. Box 176
15251 Pleasant Valley Road
Center City, MN 55012-0176
1-800-328-9000
www.hazelden.org

Illustration: David Blaisdell, Tucson, Arizona
Cover design: Kahn Design, Encinitas, California

Dedicated to:
My best friend and wife, Claudia, and my daughter Malia, my
stepson Tommy, and my father-in-law Jim. My mother,
Nannette, and father, Richard, my sister, Leslie, my brothers,
Ray and Scott, my nephews and nieces Sebastien, Emilie, Skye,
Luke, Jake, Jessie Nannette, Cairo and Kamana, and to Julie,
Tom, Fumi, Jocelyne, Richard and Stephen.

Thanks to:
David for the wonderful illustrations. I am blessed to be able to
work with him. Thanks also to Roger and Darryl for putting it
all together, almost always under deadline (usually yesterday).
Thanks to Jeff for the delightful book covers, and, even more,
for his and Pete's friendship. Thanks to Gay, Jane, Regina, Rich,
Neill and Zane for making it possible to bring these books to
life. And thanks to my mom and dad for encouraging me to
pursue my dreams.

Life is a great big canvas.
Throw all the paint you can on it.

Danny Kaye

2

3

If you keep on saying things
are going to be bad,
you have a good chance
of being a prophet.

Isaac Bashevis Singer

4

5

Trouble is a sieve through which we sift
our acquaintances. Those too big to pass
through are our friends.

Arlene Francis

7

"Where am I? Who am I?
How did I come to be here?
What is this thing called the world?
How did I come into the world?
Why was I not consulted?
And if I am compelled to take part in it,
Where is the director?
I want to see him."

Soren Kierkegaard

Don't tell me worry doesn't do any good.
I know better.
The things I worry about don't happen.

Richard M. DeVos

What a world this would be
if we just built bridges instead of walls.

Carlos Ramirez

11

The measure of a man is the size of
the thing it takes to get his goat.

12

One of my problems is that I
internalize everything. I can't express
anger, I grow a tumor instead.

Woody Allen

Fear less,hope more,
eat less, chew more,
whine less, breathe more,
talk less, say more,
hate less, love more,
and all good things will be yours.

Swedish Proverb

15

Those who bring sunshine
to the lives of others cannot
keep it from themselves.

James M. Barrie

17

Don't ask for a bigger garden,
ask only to be a better gardener.

Most people are willing to change,
not because they see the light
but because they feel the heat.

21

We are what we think.
All that we are arises with our thoughts.
With our thoughts, we make our world.

Gautama Buddha

No one can make you feel
inferior without your consent.

Eleanor Roosevelt

We do not stop playing because we are old.
We grow old because we stop playing.

25

Even a happy life cannot be without a measure of darkness and the word "happiness" would lose its meaning if it were not balanced by sadness.

C.G. Jung

27

Half the confusion in the world comes
from not knowing how little we need.

Admiral Richard E. Byrd

Little by little,
the time goes by,
short if you sing it,
long if you sigh.

I don't sing because I'm happy.
I'm happy because I sing.

William James

God always leaves
the porch light on.

32

33

If you make friends with yourself
you will never be alone.

Maxwell Maltz

35

My mother drew a distinction between achievement and success. She said that achievement is the knowledge that you have studied and worked hard and done the best that is in you. Success is being praised by others, and that's nice too, but not as important or satisfying. Always aim for achievement and forget about success.

Helen Hayes

You never lose by loving.
You always lose by holding back.

Barbara De Angelis

Our days are like identical
suitcases; all the same size, but
some people can pack more into
them than others.

P. L. Ander

It is bad to suppress laughter.
It goes back down and
spreads to your hips.

Steve Allen

40

41

There is no heavier burden
than a great potential

Charlie Brown

42

The only limit to our realization of tomorrow
will be our doubts of today.

Franklin Delano Roosevelt

People who fight fire with fire
usually end up with ashes.

Abigail Van Buren

45

Each player must accept the cards
life deals him or her. But once they
are in hand, he or she alone must
decide how to play the cards.

Voltaire

The greatest good you can do for another is
not just to share your riches,
but to reveal to him his own.

Benjamin Disraeli

The only life worth living is the adventurous life. Of such a life, the dominant characteristic is that it is unafraid. It is unafraid of what other people think . . . It does not adapt either its pace or its objectives to the pace and objectives of its neighbors. It thinks its own thoughts, reads its own books, it develops its own hopes, and it is governed by its own conscience. The herd may graze where it pleases or stampede where it pleases, but he who lives the adventurous life will remain unafraid when he finds himself alone.

Raymond B. Fosdick

When you judge someone you don't
define them, you define yourself.

Dr. Wayne Dyer

When you have got an elephant by
the hind legs and he is trying to run
away, it is best to let him run.

Abraham Lincoln

We do not always like what is good
for us in this world.

Eleanor Roosevelt

There once were four people named Everybody,
Somebody, Anybody and Nobody.
An important job had to be done, and Everybody was
sure that Somebody would do it.
Anybody could have done it, but Nobody did it.
Somebody got angry about that,
because it was Everybody's job.
Everybody thought Anybody could do it
and that Somebody would do it.
But Nobody realized that Everybody thought
Somebody would do it.
It ended up that Everybody blamed Somebody
when Nobody did what Anybody could have done.

Success Is...

Attitude, more than aptitude.

Being happy, with who you are.

Cultivating, body, mind and spirit.

Discovering, that heaven is within.

Embracing, the unknown with enthusiasm.

Facing fear, finding faith.

Giving, without remembering.

Here now, breathe into each moment.

Inside you, not in people, places or things.

Journeying, from the head to the heart.

Knowing, your beliefs create your experiences.

Letting go, and going with the flow.

Making time, for family, friends and forgiveness.

Never ever giving up, on your hopes and dreams.

Opening your heart, to magnificent possibilities.

Passion, playfulness and peace of mind.

Quiet time, the key to inspired living.

Receiving, without forgetting.

Seeking answers, questioning beliefs.

Trusting, in the beauty of your feelings and needs.

Understanding, the best you can do is always enough.

a Verb, choreograph your dance with destiny.

Willingness, to learn from everything that happens.

Xpressing yourself, be the hero of your own story.

Yours to define, how do you want to be remembered?

Zestful living, loving and laughing.

© Meiji Stewart

57

We should think seriously before
we slam doors, before we burn
bridges, before we saw off the limb
on which we find ourselves sitting.

Richard L. Evans

59

Life is what happens to us while we
are making other plans.

John Lennon

A musician must make music, an artist
must paint, a poet must write, if he is
ultimately to be at peace with himself.
What a man can be, he must be.

Albert Maslow

63

Imagination was given to man to
compensate him for what he is not,
and a sense of humor was provided
to console him for what he is.

Robert Walpole

The trouble with opportunity
is that it only knocks.
Temptation kicks the door in.

The World is a great mirror.
It reflects back to you what you are.
If you are loving, if you are friendly,
if you are helpful,
the World will prove loving and
friendly and helpful to you.
The World is what you are.

Thomas Dreier

If you go to God with a thimble,
you can only bring back a
thimbleful.

Ralph Wilkerson

This life is a test.
If it were a real life,
you would receive instructions on
where to go and what to do.

Enjoy yourself.
These are the "good old days"
you're going to miss
in the years ahead.

The grass is greener on the other side
because they mow and water the lawn.

73

The really happy person is one who
can enjoy the scenery on a detour.

DETOUR

75

Solitude is a nice place to visit,
but I wouldn't want to live there.

I do the very best I know how –
the very best I can;
and mean to keep doing so
until the end.
If the end brings me out all right,
what is said against me won't
amount to anything.
If the end brings me out wrong,
ten angels swearing I was right
would make no difference.

Abraham Lincoln

You cannot always have happiness,
but you can always give happiness.

When life gives you lemons...

81

One word or note brings more
encouragement than a thousand
thoughts...never expressed.

Christopher Morley

Do all the good you can,
in all the ways you can,
to all the souls you can
in every place you can,
at all the times you can,
with all the zeal you can,
as long as ever you can.

John Wesley

Sooner or later everyone sits down
to a banquet of consequences.

Robert Louis Stevenson

Follow the first law of holes:
if you are in one, stop digging.

Dennis Healey

87

One of the most tragic things I
know about human nature is that
all of us tend to put off living.
We are all dreaming of some
magical rose garden over the
horizon — instead of enjoying the
roses that are blooming outside our
windows today.

Dale Carnegie

89

Today is the tomorrow we
worried about yesterday,
and all is well.

I have a dream
my four little children
will one day live in a nation
where they will not be judged
by the color of their skin,
but by content of their character.

Martin Luther King, Jr.

Love people. Use things.
Not vice-versa.

Kelly Ann Rothaus

You can avoid having ulcers
by adapting to the situation:
if you fall in the mudpuddle,
check your pockets for fish.

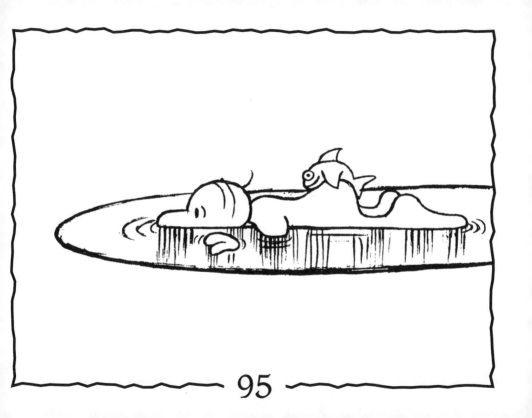

People who fly into a rage
always make a bad landing.

Will Rogers

97

You are free to choose, but the
choices you make today will
determine what you will have, be,
and do in the tomorrow of your life.

Zig Zigler

When you blame others,
you give up your power to change.

Happiness is having
a scratch for every itch.

Ogden Nash

Break through the
would's, could's and should's
in your life.

103

Why is there so much month left
at the end of the money?

The Sufis advise us to speak only
after our words have managed to
pass through three gates.
At the first we ask ourselves,
"Are these words true?"
If so, we let them pass on;
if not, back they go.
At the second gate we ask.
"Are they necessary?"
At the third gate we ask
"Are they kind?"

Ernath Easwaran

You are free to do
whatever you like.
You need only
face the consequences.

Sheldon Kopp

Straighten up your room first,
then the world.

Jeff Jordan

The world always looks brighter
from behind a smile.

STAGE

111

It takes a lot of courage to release
the familiar and seemingly secure,
to embrace the new. But there is no
real security in what is no longer
meaningful. There is more security
in the adventurous and exciting, for
in movement there is life, and in
change there is power.

Alan Cohen

There came a time when the risk
to remain tight in a bud
was more painful
than the risk it took to blossom.

Anais Nin

Never get so busy making a living
that you forget to make a life.

115

Don't hide your light
under a lampshade.

116

If you're not happy today,
what day are you waiting for?

I have learned silence from the talkative,
tolerance from the intolerant,
and kindness from the unkind.
I should not be ungrateful to those teachers.

Kahlil Gibran

The Eskimos had fifty-two names
for snow because snow was
important to them; there ought to
be as many for love.

Margaret Atwood

Sit loosely in the saddle of life.

Robert Louis Stevenson

123

Never play leapfrog with a unicorn.

125

The future never just happened.
It was created.

Will and Ariel Durant

We cannot become
what we need to be
by remaining what we are.

Max De Pree

Many things are lost
for want of asking.

English Proverb

Friends Are...

Amazing, cherish them.

Blessings, acknowledge them.

Caring, allow them.

Dependable, rely on them.

Encouraging, hear them.

Fallible, love them.

Gifts, unwrap them.

Healing, be with them.

Important, value them.

Juicy, savor them.

Kind, delight in them.

Loyal, mirror them.

Magical, soar with them.

Necessary, cultivate them.

Optimistic, support them.

Priceless, treasure them.

Quirky, enjoy them.

Rare, hold on to them.

Strong, lean on them.

Teachers, learn from them.

Understanding, talk to them.

Vulnerable, embrace them.

Warmhearted, listen to them.

Xtraordinary, recognize them.

Young At Heart, play with them.

Zany, laugh with them.

When in doubt, punt.

131

Insist on yourself;
never imitate.

Ralph Waldo Emerson

133

I still find each day too short for all
the thoughts I want to think,
all the walks I want to take,
all the books I want to read,
and all the friends I want to see.
The longer I live,the more my mind
dwells upon the beauty
and the wonder of the world.

John Burroughs

Don't hurry. Don't worry.
You're only here on a short visit,
so don't forget to
stop and smell the flowers.

Walter Hagan

To be seventy years young
is sometimes far more cheerful
than to be forty years old.

Oliver Wendell Holmes

137

The supreme happiness of life
is the conviction that we are loved.

Victor Hugo

A year from now
you may wish you
had started today.

Karen Lamb

If not you, then who?
If not now, then when?

Hillel

If you observe a really happy man, you will find him building a boat, writing a symphony, educating his son, growing double dahlias in his garden, or looking for dinosaur eggs in the Gobi desert ... He will not be striving for the goal itself. He will have become aware that he is happy in the course of living life 24 crowded hours of the day.

W. Wolfe

143

If you don't find time to exercise,
you'll have to find time for illness.

You can't leave footprints
in the sands of time
if you're sitting on your butt.
And who wants to leave buttprints
in the sands of time?

Bob Moawad

"Would you tell me please, which
way I ought to go from here?"

"That depends a good deal on where you
want to get to," said the Cat.

"I don't care where," said Alice.

"Then it doesn't matter which way
you go," said the Cat.

Lewis Carroll

Hating people is like
burning down your own house,
to get rid of a rat.

H. E. Fosdick

149

First I was dying to finish high
school and start college.
And then I was dying to finish
college and start working.
And then I was dying to
marry and have children.
And then I was dying for my
children to grow old enough for
school so I could return to work.
And then I was dying to retire.
And now I am dying...and suddenly
I realize I forgot to live.

Yesterday is history,
Tomorrow is a mystery.
Today is a gift.
That's why we call it "the present."

May you have warmth in your igloo,
oil in your lamp,
and peace in your heart.

Eskimo saying

153

Little gift books, big messages

8313

6608

6457

6456

6460

Little gift books, big messages

6458

6568

6569

6566

6570

About the Author

Meiji Stewart has created other gift books, designs, and writings that may be of interest to you. Please visit www.puddledancer.com or call 1-877-EMPATHY (367-2849) for more information about any of the items listed below.

(1) **Keep Coming Back** - Over two hundred gift products including greeting cards, wallet cards, bookmarks, magnets, bumper stickers, gift books, and more. (Free catalog available from Hazelden at 800-328-9000.)

(2) **ABC Writings** - Titles include *Children Are, Children Need, Creativity Is, Dare To, Fathers Are, Friends Are, Grandparents, Great Teachers, Happiness Is, I Am, Life Is, Loving Families, May You Always Have, Mothers Are, Recovery Is, Soulmates, Success Is,* and many more works in progress. Many of these ABC writings are available as posters (from Portal Publications) at your favorite poster and gift store, or directly from Hazelden on a variety of gift products.

(3) ***Nonviolent Communication: A Language of Compassion*** by Marshall Rosenberg. (from PuddleDancer Press) - Jack Canfield (*Chicken Soup for the Soul* author) says, "I believe the principles and techniques in this book can literally change the world – but more importantly, they can change the quality of your life with your spouse, your children, your neighbors, your co-workers, and everyone else you interact with. I cannot recommend it highly enough." Available from Hazelden and your local and on-line bookstores. For more information about The Center for Nonviolent Communication please visit www.cnvc.org.

◼ HAZELDEN®
Keep Coming Back™

Complimentary Catalog Available
Hazelden: P.O. Box 176, Center City, MN 55012-0176
1-800-328-9000   www.hazelden.org

Hazelden/Keep Coming Back titles available from your favorite bookstore:

Relax, God is in Charge	ISBN 1-56838-377-0
Keep Coming Back	ISBN 1-56838-378-9
Children are Meant to be Seen and Heard	ISBN 1-56838-379-7
Shoot for the Moon	ISBN 1-56838-380-0
When Life Gives You Lemons...	ISBN 1-56838-381-9
It's a Jungle Out There!	ISBN 1-56838-382-7
Parenting... Part Joy... Part Guerrilla Warfare	ISBN 1-56838-383-5
God Danced the Day You Were Born	ISBN 1-56838-384-3
Happiness is an Inside Job	ISBN 1-56838-385-1
Anything is Possible	ISBN 1-56838-386-X

Acknowledgements

Every effort has been made to find the copyright owner of the material used.
However, there are a few quotations that have been impossible to trace, and we
would be glad to hear from the copyright owners of these quotations, so that
acknowledgement can be recognized in any future edition.